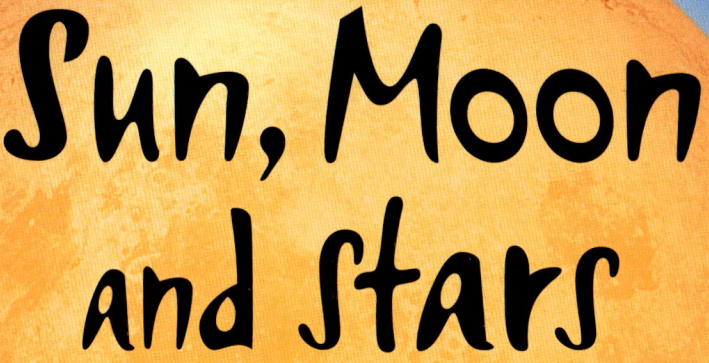

Sun, Moon and Stars

Stephanie Turnbull
Designed by Zöe Wray

Illustrated by Kuo Kang Chen and Uwe Mayer

Space consultant: Stuart Atkinson

Reading consultant: Alison Kelly,
Roehampton University

Contents

3	The night sky	20	Vanishing trick
4	Out in space	22	Stars
6	The Sun	24	Star groups
8	Earth and Sun	26	Shooting stars
10	Nearby planets	28	Space watch
12	Faraway planets	30	Glossary of space words
14	The Moon		
16	A rocky desert	31	Websites to visit
18	Moon missions	32	Index

The night sky

When you look at the night sky, you can see shining stars, far away in space.

You might be able to spot the Moon too.

Everything you can see is only a tiny part of space.

The Moon looks small, but it would take about four days to drive all the way around it.

Out in space

Our planet Earth is a lump of rock in space. It is one of a group of nine planets.

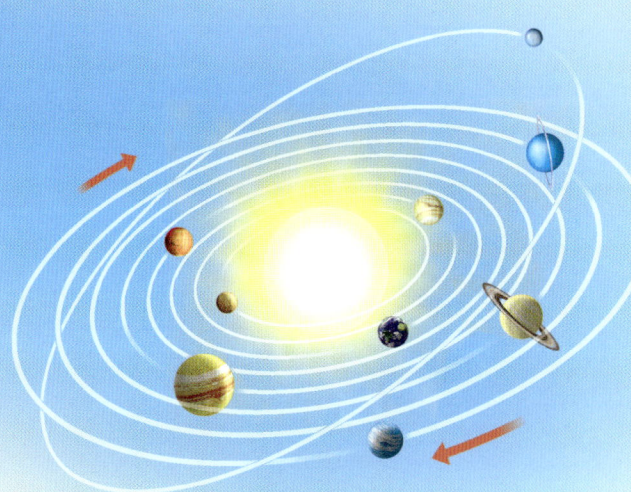

Each planet goes around the Sun on its own invisible path.

The Sun and the planets are called the Solar System.

Mars

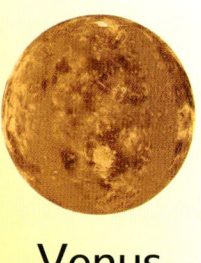
Earth

Venus

Sun

Mercury

Experts used to think that Pluto was a planet, but now they've changed their minds and call it a dwarf planet.

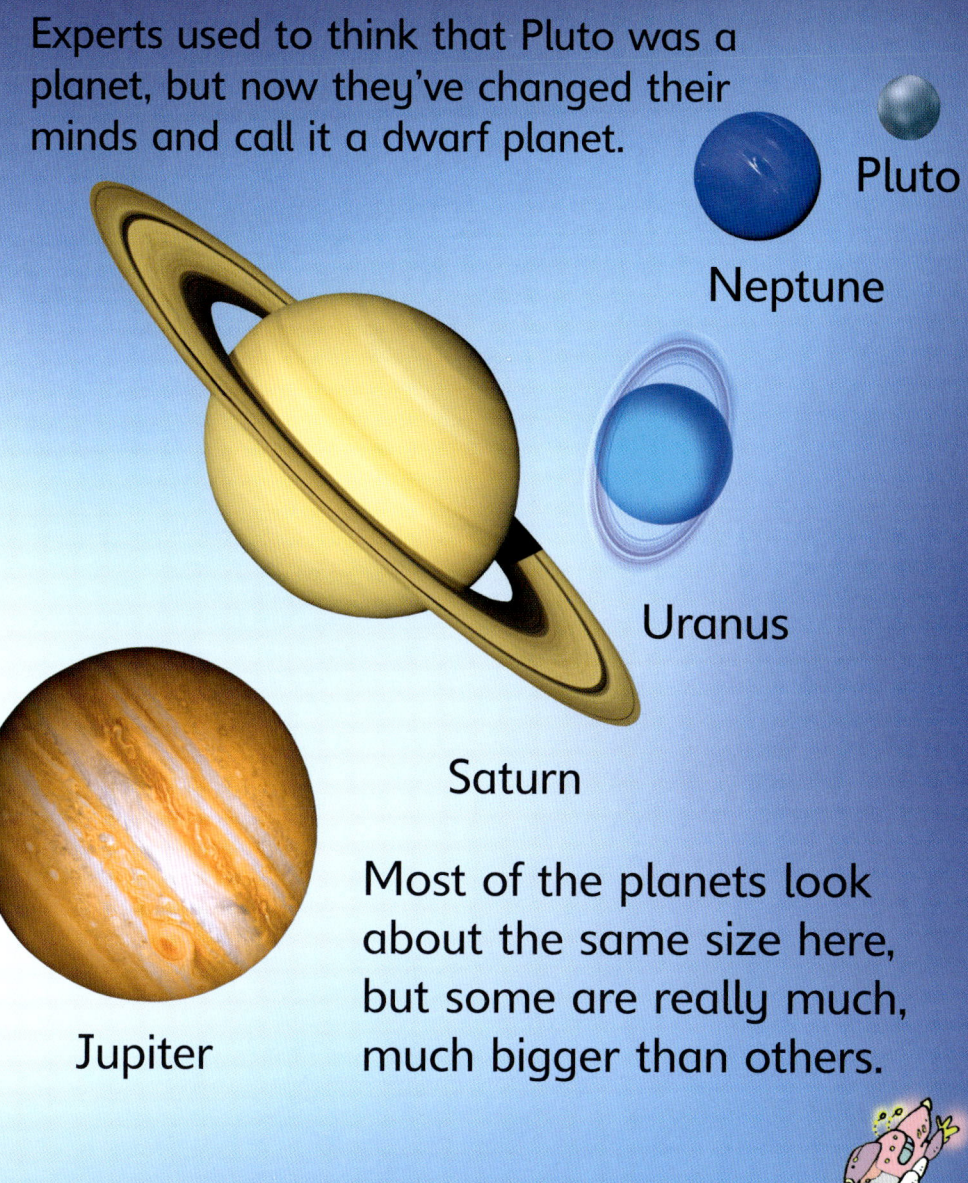

Pluto

Neptune

Uranus

Saturn

Jupiter

Most of the planets look about the same size here, but some are really much, much bigger than others.

Saturn is so far away from Earth that it took seven years for a spacecraft to reach it.

The Sun

The Sun is a star. It is the closest star to Earth, so it looks bigger than other stars.

The Sun was formed by thick clouds of dust and gas.

It became a glowing ball of gas that is hottest in the middle.

The surface of the Sun bubbles and boils.

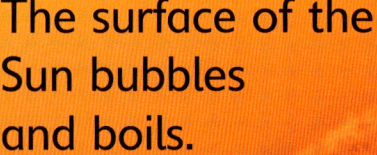

Sunspot —

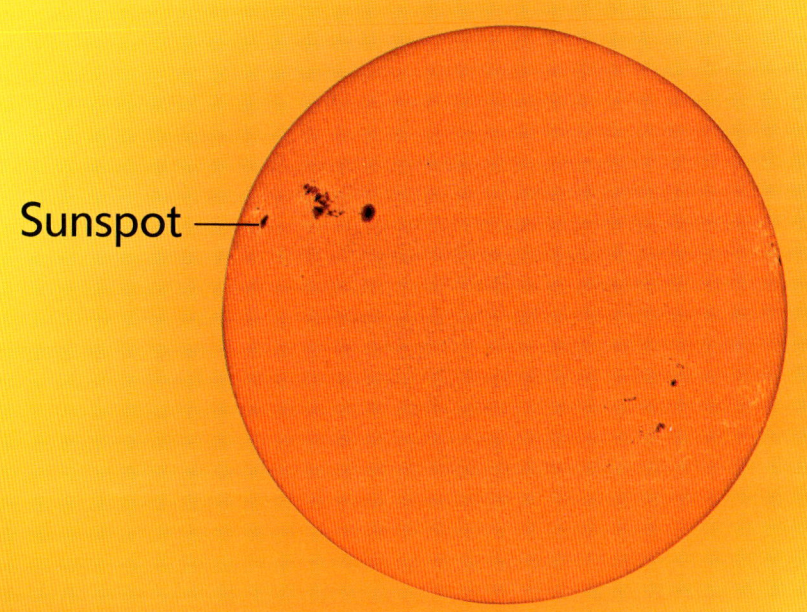

The Sun has dark areas called sunspots. They are cooler than the rest of the Sun.

Never look straight at the Sun. Its strong light can hurt your eyes.

Earth and Sun

Earth turns as it moves around the Sun.

The parts of Earth facing the Sun have day. Parts that light doesn't reach have night. As Earth turns, different parts have day or night.

When it gets dark where you live, it is just getting light on the other side of Earth.

The Sun is a long way away from Earth. A spacecraft called Ulysses studies the Sun from space.

It can't fly too close to the Sun, because it would melt in the heat.

The Sun gives us light and heat. No plants or animals could live without it.

Nearby planets

The four planets closest to the Sun are Mercury, Venus, Earth and Mars.

They are all rocky planets, but Earth is the only one that plants and animals live on.

This is Venus. It has high mountains and volcanoes. The planet's air is poisonous.

 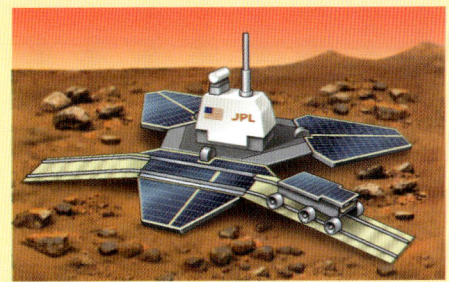

A few years ago, a small spacecraft was sent to Mars.

The spacecraft opened up and a robot car drove out.

The car was about the size of a skateboard. Scientists on Earth used computers to make it move and take photos.

Mercury is so close to the Sun that the land is hotter than boiling water.

Faraway planets

Jupiter, Saturn, Uranus and Neptune are far away from the Sun. They are very cold places.

Jupiter is the biggest planet in the Solar System.

This red spot on Jupiter is a storm that is about twice the size of Earth.

Saturn has bright rings around it.

 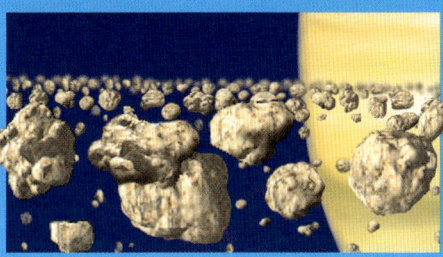

From far away, Saturn's rings look like solid hoops.

In fact each ring is made up of dust, rocks and ice.

The surface of dwarf planet Pluto is frozen, like a huge skating rink.

The Moon

The Moon is a ball of rock that goes around and around the Earth.

As the Moon moves, the Sun lights up different parts of it. This is why the Moon seems to change shape in the night sky.

When the Sun shines behind the Moon, you can't see its light side. It is called a New Moon.

Sometimes you can only see part of the Moon. This is called a Crescent Moon.

When the Sun lights up the whole side of the Moon, you can see a Full Moon.

Other planets have moons too. Jupiter has more than 40 moons.

A rocky desert

The Moon is a dry, dusty place. It has no air or water, so nothing lives there.

The Moon's surface is rocky and hilly. It is covered in giant holes called craters.

Crater

Many of the Moon's craters are so big that whole cities could fit inside them.

There are lots of rocks drifting in space.

Sometimes a rock crashes into the Moon.

The rock explodes and dust flies everywhere.

It makes a deep, bowl-shaped crater.

Moon missions

The Moon is the only place in space where people have landed. This is how astronauts got there.

1. A rocket blasted off into space, with astronauts inside.

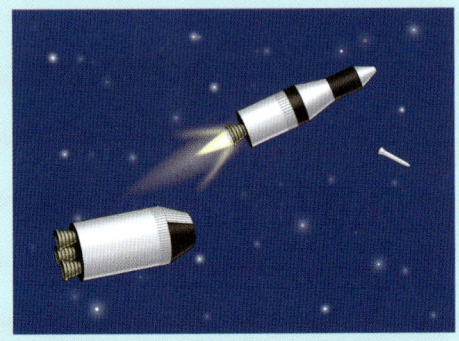

2. Parts of the rocket fell away, leaving a small spacecraft.

3. A lunar module came out and landed on the Moon.

4. Astronauts climbed down the ladder onto the Moon's surface.

Astronauts explored the Moon in an electric car. They collected rocks to bring back.

This is a piece of rock from the Moon.

In the future, scientists might build special hotels on the Moon for people to stay in.

Vanishing trick

Sometimes the Moon moves in front of the Sun and blocks out the Sun's light. This is called a solar eclipse.

This black circle is the Moon, covering the Sun. Gases from the Sun glow around the edges.

At the start of an eclipse, the Sun looks as if it has a bite taken out of it.

As the Moon covers more of the Sun, the sky gets darker and it feels colder.

The Moon covers the Sun completely for a short time.

During an eclipse, many animals think it must be night, so they get ready to sleep.

Stars

Stars are glowing balls of gas, like the Sun.

The bright star in this photo is much bigger than the Sun, but it looks small because it is so far away.

Some stars slowly get bigger and duller over many years.

They puff off layers of gas and slowly fade away.

Many stars move around in pairs. They are called double stars.

Some big stars explode. This cloud of gas is all that's left of an exploded star.

Star groups

Stars can be joined up to make patterns.

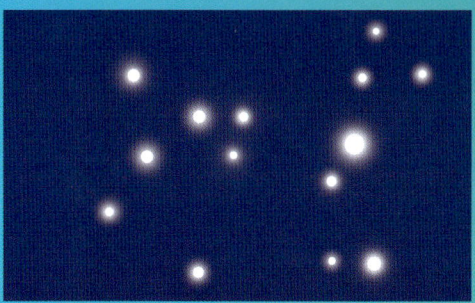

This pattern of stars is called the Great Dog.

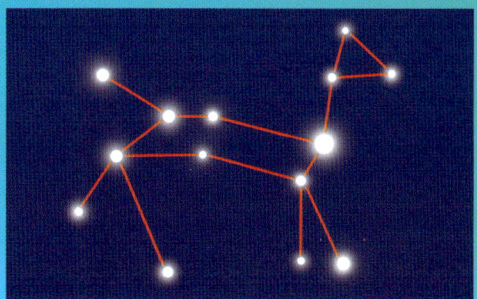

If lines join the stars, you can see a dog shape.

A group of billions of stars is called a galaxy. One galaxy is called the Whirlpool because of its swirling shape.

The Whirlpool galaxy

Most galaxies are spiral or oval shapes. One galaxy looks like a wheel.

Shooting stars

A shooting star is not really a star. It is a small, hot piece of space rock.

Shooting stars are also known as meteors. They look like stars falling out of the sky.

Often lots of space rocks fall at once. This is called a meteor shower.

Space rocks heat up if they come too near Earth.

They burn away, leaving a trail of light behind them.

Some rocks are too big to burn up, so they hit Earth. This huge crater was made by a rock that fell in Arizona, U.S.A.

Space watch

People use telescopes to look at space.
They make things look bigger and clearer.

This huge telescope floats around Earth.
It takes photos and sends them back to Earth.

A spacecraft took the telescope into space.

A robot arm lifted the telescope out.

At first the telescope didn't work properly. Astronauts had to go into space to fix it.

You can see faraway planets, stars and whole galaxies through powerful telescopes.

Glossary of space words

Here are some of the words in this book you might not know. This page tells you what they mean.

 planet - a huge round object in space. Earth is a planet.

 Solar System - the Sun and the nine planets that go around it.

 crater - a hole on the Moon or a planet, made by a space rock hitting it.

 astronaut - a person who is specially trained to travel into space.

 lunar module - a small spacecraft that landed on the Moon.

 galaxy - a group of billions of stars. There are millions of galaxies in space.

 telescope - something that makes things far away look bigger and closer.

Websites to visit

You can visit exciting websites to find out more about sun, moon and stars.

To visit these websites, go to the Usborne Quicklinks website at **www.usborne.com/quicklinks** Read the internet safety guidelines, and then type the keywords "**beginners sun**".

The websites are regularly reviewed and the links in Usborne Quicklinks are updated. However, Usborne Publishing is not responsible, and does not accept liability, for the content or availability of any website other than its own. We recommend that children are supervised while on the internet.

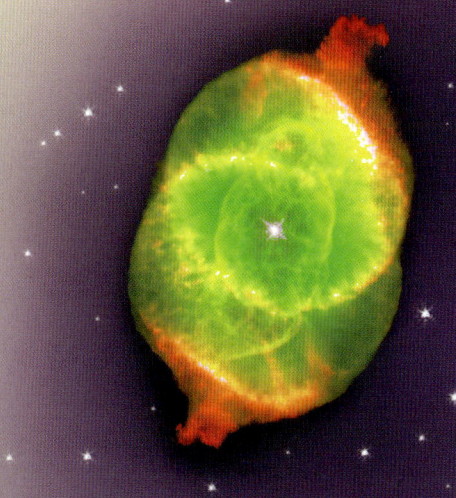

This is a photo of the Cat's Eye Nebula. It was taken through a powerful telescope.

Index

astronauts, 18, 19, 29, 30
craters, 16, 17, 27, 30
Earth, 4, 5, 6, 8, 9, 10, 28
galaxies, 24-25, 30
Jupiter, 5, 12, 15
lunar module, 18, 30
Mars, 4, 10, 11
Mercury, 4, 10, 11
meteors, 26-27
Moon, 3, 14-15, 16-17, 18-19, 20, 21
Neptune, 5, 12
planets, 4-5, 10-11, 12-13, 30
Pluto, 5, 12, 13
Saturn, 5, 12, 13
shooting stars, 26-27
solar eclipse, 20-21
Solar System, 4-5, 12, 30
spacecraft, 5, 9, 11, 18, 28
space rocks, 17, 26, 27
stars, 3, 6, 22-23, 24-25
Sun, 4, 6-7, 8, 9, 10, 14, 15, 20, 21, 22
telescopes, 28-29, 30
Ulysses, 9
Uranus, 5, 12
Venus, 4, 10

Acknowledgements

Cover design: Nicola Butler
Photographic manipulation by Emma Julings and John Russell

Photo credits

The publishers are grateful to the following for permission to reproduce material:
© **Alamy** 2-3 (Doug Steley), 16 (Pictor International); © **Corbis** 1 (Myron Jay Dorf), 8 (Roger Ressmeyer), 27 (Charles & Josette Lenars); © **David A. Hardy** 9 (astroart.org); © **Digital Vision** Cover (Earth); © **ESO/NASA** 22-23, 24-25, 30 (galaxy); © **NASA** Cover (Moon), 4-5, 6-7, 14, 15, 19, 28, 29, 31; © **Science Photo Library** 10 (David P. Anderson, SMU/NASA), 11 & 12 (NASA), 13, 20 (Chris Butler)

Every effort has been made to trace and acknowledge ownership of copyright. If any rights have been omitted, the publishers offer to rectify this in any subsequent editions following notification.

First published in 2003 by Usborne Publishing Ltd., Usborne House, 83-85 Saffron Hill, London EC1N 8RT, England. www.usborne.com Copyright © 2007, 2003 Usborne Publishing Ltd. The name Usborne and the devices ⚏⊛ are Trade Marks of Usborne Publishing Ltd. All rights reserved. No part of this publication may be reproduced, stored in a retrieval system, or transmitted in any form or by any means, electronic, mechanical, photocopying, recording or otherwise without the prior permission of the publisher.
First published in America 2003. U.E. Printed in China.